EUGENIO PUCCI

W9-BGG-715

POMPEII

PRACTICAL GUIDE FOR THE VISIT TO THE EXCAVATIONS

3 Itineraries

BONECHI - EDIZIONI "IL TURISMO"
5, VIA DEI RUSTICI - FIRENZE

Welcome
to Pompeii

I should like to offer you a cordial and hospitable welcome, then to thank you for having made the journey here after having seen the wonders of Naples and its environs. You have come from a city and places where Nature and art have completely enthralled you, so it is understandable if you come to Pompeii in another frame of mind, with much curiosity and perhaps even with sodness. Visiting the so-called « dead city », the unearthed city, can evoke a feeling of sadness and of religious awe; however, contrary to all your expectations, following step by step the guide which we have written for you, you ill realize, almost magically, that the city is alive, fascinating, full of unexpecied surprises, even if sometimes jou are reminded harshly of the Pompeian tragedy.

We have tried to make your visit quicker and easier, and to explain the excavations even in the smallest particulars, especially in regard to the archeological terminology, the variety of the painting and architectural styles, and with the description of the civic, religious and domestic customs we hope to have made you familiar with those far-off times. We trust we have succeeded in this aim, and when you leave the archeological boundaries which for a few hours have made you most welcome guests of ancient Pompeii, we are sure that you will keep our guide as a pleasant souvenir of Pompeii, Naples and Italy.

THE EDITOR

SUBIECT INDEX

COMMUNICATIONS FROM NAPLES AND USEFUL INFORMATION

The excavations at Pompeii are usually reached from Naples by one of the following routes. The journey by State Railways takes at least 40 minutes, and a maximum of an hour (either by « diretto » or « accelerato »), and the station is near the Porta Marina, from where the tours often start. The electric train « Circumvesuviana » leaves from the Station at Naples in Corso Garibaldi, on the right as you face the Railway Station in Piazza Garibaldi. You should ask for a ticket for Pompeii-Scavi, and the journey should take 30 minutes (« diretto ») or 45 minutes (« accelerato »), entering the excavations by the Porta di Nola. It is 22 km. from Naples to Pompeii on the Autostrada, and the journey by car or bus to Porta Marina would take little more than half and hour. The Circumvesuviana also stops at Pompeii Nuovo (New Pompeii), the town which has grown up around the famous Sanctuary of the Madonna of the Rosary, the goal of many throngs of pilgrims. To reach ancient Pompeii, take the road to the right, and after a short journey of about 10 minutes you will come to a semi-circular « piazza » (square). Your visit begins with a view of the great amphitheatre on the right, and on the left the Palestra (Gymnasium), and the entrance to the new excavations and to the Via dell'Abbondanza. The excavations may be inspected from 9 a.m. until an hour before sunset.

It should be noted that from July 1 to September 30 the most important sections of the buildings are illuminated from 8 p.m. to 11 p.m., offering a beautiful spectacle to any evening visitors who, entering by the Porta Marina, will be allowed to visit the Antiquarium, the Forum and the various buildings sorrounding it, the Stabian Baths, part of the Via dell'Abbondanza, the Via dei Teatri with the Great and Little Theatres, and the Gladiators' Quarters. Through the Porta di Stabia, in the Viale dei Teatri, is the *Auditorium*, where lectures and illustrated talks on the excavations are held for Italian and foreign tourist. In the summer season there are musical and dramatic productions in the Pompeian theatres in the area. Information both on the lectures and the other performances can be obtained in the press and from travel and tourist agencies.

On the map of the excavations the itinerary suggested by this guide is numbered consecutively from 1 to 57, and if you follow it exactly you will have inspected the entire area which has been excavated. However, this itinerary requires a great deal of time, since a visit just to the excavations enclosed within the surrounding walls of the « unearthed » city would take more than 5 hours; and at a short distance is the Villa dei Misteri (Villa of the Mysteries), which can be reached by car or cab. For those with little time at their disposal, we suggest the following three itineraries, with the numbers which should be followed on the map.

FIRST ITINERARY (an hour and a half).
no. 1, 3, 4, 5, 8, 12, 13, 14, 15, 21, 22, 23.

SECOND ITINERARY (two hours and a half).
no. 1, 3, 4, 5, 8, 9, 10, 11, 12, 13, 14, 15, 21, 22, 23, 33, 38, 40, 41.

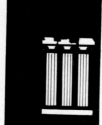

THIRD ITINERARY (three hours and a half).
no. 1, 2, 4, 5, 8, 9, 10, 11, 12, 13, 14, 15, 21, 23, 33, 38, 40, 41, 42, 43, 44, 45, 46, 47, 48, 49, 50, 51, 52, 53, 54.

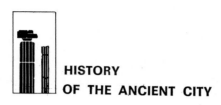

HISTORY
OF THE ANCIENT CITY

It is impossible to say definitely what was the origin of ancient Pompeii. Even its name is uncertain. It has not been established whether it was of Greek or Italic derivation, however the accepted version is that must have come from the Greek « pémpo, pompé » or from the Oscan « pompe », while the city is probably Oscan, since this was the principal race in Campania. What we know for a certainty dates back to the 6th. century B.C., as the town was already in existence, with its primitive urban centre surrounded by solid walls; however it is undeniable that it must have existed since before the 8th. century B.C., at least as a rather small centre consisting of people concerned with agriculture, scattered about the valley of the Sarno. We can presume this from its pre-eminent geographic position, since Pompeii is situated on the heights, and looks out over the plain where the river runs toward the sea, providing a landing-place for the daring Greek and Phoenician navigators who wanted to increase their trade.

The Greeks, who were firmly established at Cumae, thus controlling all the gulf of Naples as far as Sorrento, Capri and Ischia, were the people who above all had an eye on Pompeii. The opportunity of bringing it within the orbit of the powerful State of Cumae was provided by the hostility of the Etruscans, who controlled the Campanian hinterland. In order to survive, Pompeii was forced to ally itself commercially and politically with the Greeks of Cumae. But the Etruscans soon knew of this, and regained their lost position between 525 B.C. and 474 B.C. This was, however, only for a short time, because their fleet was defeated by the Greeks, and the city returned under Greek hegemony.

The Pompeians were not organized to defend themselves against the Etruscans and Greeks, and thus could not expect to live independently. So when in the 5th. century B.C. the Samnites, coming from Hirpinia and Samnium, scattered the Greeks and Etruscans, Pompeii was obliged to submit to a new master. From then on not only was the city governed according to Samnite customs, laws and habits, but it also absorbed its language and religion. Little is known of life in the town during the period of Samnite supremacy, but it could not have been very peaceful, as in 310 B.C. the Pompeians and the Nucerians had to take up arms to defend themselves against the attacks of the Roman fleet, which used to disembark its men at the mouth of the Sarno, and marauded the coast.

When Rome became powerful she conquered the Samnites, and Pompeii was forced to accept a particular sort of association which allowed her a certain independence. However in the period of the Social Wars, initiated by the Italians against Rome, Pompeii decided to throw off the yoke, and fought to regain her liberty, but Rome, after many vicissitudes, conquered the Italians at Nola, and Pompeii from thenceforth became known officially as Colonia Cornelia Veneria (c. 80 B.C.). It was not an easy task for the Romans to subdue so many different elements in the political, economic and social character of the town, but as time passed the Pompeians became completely « Romanised », to the extent of accepting the language, customs, legislation and municipal arrangements of the Quirites.

Tacitus comments on the character of the Pompeians of that time, in his Annals, when he describes the tragic and terrible brawl which broke out between the Pompeians and the Nucerians, during a performance by Gladiators in the Amphitheatre, in 59 A.D. Two pairs of gladiators (one local and one from Nuceria) were fighting each other in the arena, and their display sent delirious the crowd of spectators, who, as always happens in any competitive sport, supported one side or the other. Apparently one of the fans of the town team made some deprecating remark about the adversaries' team, and then the argument, which degenerated into a general brawl, ended with the massacre of as many Nucerians as came under the hands of the Pompeians. When the facts were known at Rome and related by Nero to the Senate, a severe punishment was imposed: the Amphitheatre was closed for ten years.

The first premonition of disaster was the terrible earthquake of 62 A.D. Like many other cities in Campania, Pompeii suffered heavy damage, but once the fear of a further disturbance had passed, work was begun with alacrity on the reconstruction and restoration of the temples and the public and private buildings. The city was enriched with new aristocratic mansions, workshops, and shops, increasing its economic, commercial and industrial strength.

But seventeen years later, on August 24, 79 A.D., a little after midday, the horrible disaster occurred: Vesuvius erupted and literally interred the city, (together with Herculaneum, and Stabia) under a layer of ashes, « lapilli » (small pieces of pumice) and other substance from the eruption, to a depth of between 19 and 23 feet. Hardly anyone could escape. A great part of the population, which must then have been about 20,000 souls, died soflocated in the streets, in the houses and underground, where many thought to escape from the destructive fury of the fire and the noxious fumes. Plaster casts taken from the spaces left by the bodies of humans, interred under the hard skin of ashes and « lapilli », are grim evidence of their terrible agony. Pliny the Elder hastened to help the Pompeians from the base at Misenum. He, besides being an admiral, could also claim to be a learned scholar of natural phenomena, but he could do nothing, unfortunately, before death overtook him during his humane and scientific investigations. What we do know of the eruption has come down to us from his nephew, Pliny the Younger, in two dramatic letters sent to Tacitus.

As time passed, and there were further eruptions at Pompeii, no one could discover the exact location of the city, despite the letters of Pliny's nephew. Even when the architect Domenico Fontana, while constructing a canal to carry water from the Sarno to Torre Annunziata, discovered ruins and inscriptions, it could not be established that these were from Pompeii. In 1748 Charles of Bourbon initiated excavations but these were more concerned with tunnels to take objects and statues from the houses. During the Napoleonic era greater efforts were made, and between 1815 and 1932 were discovered the Forum, the House of the Faun, the House of Pansa, and the smaller Baths, then the Stabian Baths came to light in the years 1850-59.

When the Kingdom of Italy was formed, in 1860, the supervision of the excavations was entrusted to Giuseppe Fiorelli, who began his excellent work following a strictly scientific method. It was his brilliant inspiration to obtain casts of the victims and of various wooden furnishings by pouring liquid plaster through holes into the spaces left in the bed of ashes. After Fiorelli followed other distinguished students of archaeology, perfecting the methods of excavation: Michele Ruggiero, Giulio de Petra, Antonio Sogliano and Vittorio Spinazzola. But the man who brought the excavations to their present stage, bringing to light at least three-fifths of the area of the city, was the world-famous Professor Amedeo Maiuri, who worked there from 1924. Those interested in investigating more thoroughly every secret of archaeological excavations in Campania should refer to his numerous essays and bound volumes. For Pompeii and Herculaneum we recommend the beautiful book the famous archaeologist published in 1959: « Pompei ed Ercolano fra case e abitanti » (Publisher: Aldo Martello).

LAY OUT OF THE CITY

As the deep cover of ashes and « lapilli » has gradually been removed, a particular urban structure which is not found in any other Roman city was revealed to archeologists and to posterity. Pompeii, as we mentioned in the historical notes, was dominated by various rulers:

View of Pompeii seen from the Street of Mercury.

Etruscans, Greeks, Samnites and Romans, apart from the primitive Italic people who must have constituted the first city core where the Forum now stands. The city has thus undergone several urban experiments, which can all be recognized by the various construction materials and techniques used by the various rulers. Thus five distinct periods of construction can be noted; Pre-Samnite, from the 6th. and 5th. centuries B.C.; Samnite, from the 4th. and 3rd. centuries; the second Samnite period under Greek influence, 200-80 B.C.; the first Roman period, 80 B.C. to 14 A.D., Republican and Augustan; the second Roman period, 14-79 A.D., the Claudian and Flavian period. Each of these epochs had its own methods of construction, using different materials and using them according to experience acquired. It is from this that investigators have been able to establish definitely the various phases of the transformation of the city and its buildings.

Naturally, the greatest influence is that of the Republican and Imperial era, but the particular conformation of the land led to a departure from the prototype of the « city on a square », according to the dictares of the urban Quirites. The city rises on a spur of land which was originally prehistoric lava, about 40 metres above sea-level, and the city-planners had to work according to the demands of the terrain, as there is a not inconsiderable slope from north to south, while the flat area is at the extreme west limit of the city. It is fact on these flat areas that most important public zuildings are situated, while the real city centre is completely covered by the houses grouped into islands making rectilineal blocks, with streets crossing at right angles, and bordered by narrow foot-paths, with a fountain at the intersection. A later development was the placement of large stones to assist the pedestrian trying to cross.

It two areas at the farthest limits of the inhabited area can be found the triangular Forum and the Theatres, in the southern sector, while in that of the south- esat are the Great Amphitheatre and the Palestra (Gymnasium). The fortifying walls stretch 3 km. 22 m., and the built-up area covers about 161 acres.

One of the most vivid cheracteristics of the city is the abundant epigraphy: inscriptions which constitute a truly vivid element of city life. As the excavations proceeded it was necessary to collate and decipher these inscriptions scratched or painted on the plaster walls, so that they could be recorded, since bad weather or other causes could erase them forever. Most of the wall inscriptions were painted in large red or black letters, or else scratched with a stylus in normal characters. These « graffiti » wece usually some form of publicity, referring to events at the Amphitheatre; or « For Rent » notices, and those about lost property; propaganda urging the citizens at election time to vote for this or that candidate; or information about workshops and taverns. They are often found in shops, amphi-theatres, houses; in the places most frequented by a heterogeneous crowd; there are reminders of debts, moneys received, declarations of love, obscene phrases, caricatures, dates to remember for private affairs. This is also one of the most interesting aspects of the « dead city », as we so often term Pompeii. But the title is wrong, since ancient Pompeii is alive now for us and for posterity, with evidence of the life which the dreadful disaster suddenly interrupted; and which comes again into the light, reappearing in a spectacular manner, almost as if it were a genuine revival, which endures for the benefit of millions of visitors, who will spread throughout the world the story of the history and civilisation of Pompeii.

12

A HOUSE IN POMPEII
AND ITS DECORATION

What we have said about the urban structure can also apply to the town buildings. Each epoch has left its mark, and we shall observe this as we proceed on our visit. Since the Roman element predominates in the architecture, illustrated is a plan of the famous *House of the Vettii*, giving a clear idea of the structure of the interior, and of the various areas into which the majority of aristocratic hauses were divided. We should also become familiar with the terminology for each section, since these terms will be used on each occasion we deal with a new building, and the visitor can refer to this plan when we enter the house itself.

First of all, the Roman house was enclosed within high, window-less walls, and could almost be called a small fortress; from outside no-one could see anything, and the inhabitants of the house could enjoy complete privacy. The following are the names of the various sections: (1) *vestibulum*: the space in front of the entrance door, projecting beyond the surrounding wall, and thus named because it as sacred to the goddess Vesta; (2) *fauces*: the passage leading to the atrium; (3) *atrium*: rectangular room from which open the other rooms of the house. This could be considered the busiest part of the house, since domestic life revolved around it. (In other houses in front of the atrium was the *tablinum,* where the head of the house once used to reside, but which later became a reception-room.) With the passing of time the atrium began to resemble a courtyard, covered by a roof supported by pillars and columns, thus becoming a portico which was termed *tetrastyle* if thete were four columns, one at each corner, and *Corinthian* if the columns were more numerous. Rainwater came in through the open space, the *compluvium*, and was collected in the *impluvium* (9), the basin in the middle of the *atrium.* From the atrium we pass to the *peristyle* (4 and 7), the large courtyard surrounded by porticoes, with the orchard or garden with fountains and statues (5) inside. Next were the *cubicula* (6), the rooms used as bed-rooms; the *triclinium* (8, 13, 16, 17) or dining-room, with the three couches (clinai) on which the diners reclined, around three sides of the table, leaving the fourth free for service. It is interesting to notice that in the houses of the aristocracy several « triclinari » or living-rooms are disposed in different parts of the house. Thus throughout the various seasons there was always a living-room where fresh air and the sunshine could be enjoyed. The *alae* (14) are usually the two rooms found at each end of the atrium; they were used as store-rooms, or sometimes housed the « Lararium », the shrine or small chapel where the sacred things of the house were kept, or in them were painted representations of the divinities,

13

Love Punished. (Naples, National Museum).

objects of worship. In the houses of the rich, paintings of ancestors were kept in the *ala*. Lastly, the *oecus*, the private apartments of the house.

In both the houses and in the public buildings various architectural orders can be found, as follows: *Doric*, *Ionic*, *Corinthian* and *Tuscan*. The *Doric* order can be distinguished by the column gradually tapering from the base upwards, decorated with vertical fluting, with a square capital with sharp corners. The *Ionic* order has the column supported on a base, and prolific fluting divided by cintures, and the capital has two circular volutes or scrolls. The *Corinthian* order has the capital decorated with leaves of the acanthus (a herbaceous plant with large irregular shaped leaves) under the Ionic volutes. The *Tuscan* order was used in rustic buildings; the columns had no grooves and the base was solid. The so-called *Composite* order can also be found; it is derived from the fusion of Corinthian and Ionic elements.

Roman houses were not always identical to this, often we find them fronted by shops or taverns, depending on the business of the inhabitants. However we can still find at Pompeii other examples of houses of the primitive austere type which gradually began to be modified by the influence of Hellenic and Roman taste. Houses and aristocratic villas are enriched by artistic furnishings, paintings, mosaics and small bronze and marble sculptures. These features demonstrate the extent of the development not only of real artists, but also of the artisans whose imagination had free rein in the

Marine Life (Naples. National Museum).

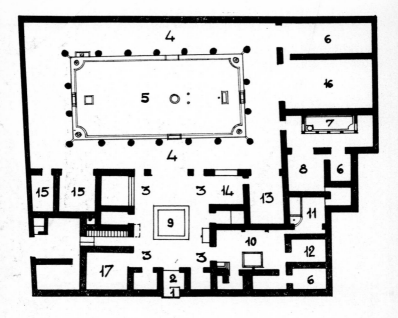

HOUSE OF THE VETTII.

1. - Vestibulum
2. - Fauces
3. - Atrium
4. - Peristyle
5. - Garden
6. - Cubicula
7. - Peristyle
8. - Triclinium

9. - Impluvium
10. - Hall with a Lararium
11. 12. - Kitchen
13. - Triclinium
14. - Alae
15. - Oecus
16. 17. - Triclinium

production of everyday objects, bronze plate and precious silverware. Above all, painting should be remembered, since when one speaks of Roman painting it is almost exclusively with reference to the mural paintings in Pompeii and Herculaneum. These paintings, up till now have been considered the extremely competent efforts of craftsmen, and above all as an authentic derivation — if not an actual imitation — of ancient Hellenic painting; but the sensitive observer will not hesitate to recognize in the various paintings the expert hand of artists from the country, of high quality. This observation refers particularly to the frescoes of the Villa of the Mysteries, and many others of high quality which are now in the Archeological Museum in Naples, which demonstrate the style of the various artists, despite the fact that they are anonymous.

Venus and Mars. (Naples, National Museum).

This type of wall painting can be divided into 4 styles: the *first style* is termed « incrustation » (inlay), because the surface of the stucco walls is divided into coloured rectangles, imitating marble inlay. This style, which is reminiscent of the Hellenic mode, died out towards the end of the 1st. century B.C. Characteristic of the *second style* is « architecture in perspective », that is, various architectural elements like plinths, columns, architraves, cornices and porticoes were painted on the walls to that they seemed to project towards the observer. In the spaces enclosed by these elements were landscapes or imaginative designs. This style was in vogue from the

17

Battle of Issus, detail of Darius. (Naples, National Museum).

first half of the Ist. century B.C. until half-way through the first century A.D. The *third style*, called « the actual wall », evolved from the second, except there is no longer any perspective, and the walls assume the function of tapestries or ornamental carpets. The third style developed in the period of the reign of Augustus, and seems to have been influenced by Egyptian art, after Egypt became a Roman province in the year 30 BC. The *fourth style* is called « architectural illusionism », and is almost a return to the second style, but can be distinguished from it because the architectural elements are depicted with improbable fineness, giving rise to fantastic scenes rich in the most vivid colours. The fourth style was in fashion in the second half of the 1st. century A. D., and is the predominating style at Pompeii.

We said that the Roman painting at Pompeii has above all an illustrative value; in fact its compositions on mythological subjects can all be considered as imitations of Greek originals. Thus is preserved the echo of a tradition of painting which has not reached us. The Pompeian wall-paintings are executed in fresco, tempera and encausto. The « a fresco » painting is done on a plaster of fresh lime, with the colours crushed and diluted in water; the « a tempera » method uses colours diluted in a glutinous and gummy substance,

The three Graces (Naples, National Museum).

20

with egg yolk and wax; the « encausto » is obtained by mixing the colours in wax, and then heating the paint (« encautizzato ») so that the wax penetrates the colours and fixes them. The artists used to paint their fantasies on the wall using one colour as a base, usually pink or yellow, but sometimes black, green and blue.

Roman artists did not like only large compositions; the Pompeians also enjoyed decorating the living areas of their houses, villas and palaces with everyday scenes, fantastic sights, still life, literary and romantic subjects, and also often with extremely vivid portraits. In Roman portraiture it can already be seen that the artist is no longer under Greek influence, but deliberately adheres to an entirely personal interpretation which is expressed in the numerous scenes and sketches in popular style which can found everywhere in Pompeii. We can compare the painting with mosaic decoration, which is found in the houses of the aristocracy, but is also present, in more modest form, in the houses of the poor. This decoration is used lavishly either on the walls or on the floor. Various mosaic forms can be recognized: those with black and white designs on a monochrome base are termed « opus Alexandrinum »; the « opus tessellatum » has the small pieces in straight lines along the sides; and those with the lines curved are called « opus vermiculatum ». The technique of the « opus signinum » was to mix the small coloured pieces without any attempt at a pattern, and in the « opus sectile » the mosaic pieces are cut to fit into the arrangement of the design. Pompeian mosaic decoration presents a wide range of geometrical outlines, designs inspired by the animal and plant world, hunting scenes, battles and sporting activities.

THE TRAGIC
FORTUNE OF POMPEII

We show here the tragic but fortunate Vesuvius. Tragic because of the eruptions which caused the apocalyptic calamity of the destruction of entire cities like Pompeii, Herculaneum and Stabia, yet fortunate for us because she has preserved her victims almost intact, a silent yet eloquent testimony of a not inglorious past, of an industrious way of life, of a civilization on display for us in its most intimate essence. In the Forum, looking towards the Temple of Jupiter, you find her before you, immense, grey, with her two peaks (Somma and Vesuvius) about 1270 metres high. After the last eruption in 1944 (the photograph was taken during these eruptions) Vesuvius seems to be dormant, and the famous plume, so beloved by good Neapolitans, has disappeared. Let us hope her sleep lasts thousands of years. The very barrenness, caused by the rivers of lava and ashes, evokes respect mixed with fear. But Vesuvius has not always been like this, in fact before the terrible eruption of 79 A.D. the summit was covered with woods, where the hairy wild boar preyed on game of all species, while the slopes down to the plain were covered with luxuriant vineyards. The delicious Vesuvian wine, of which the Pompeians were very proud, was kept by them in wine flasks with the inscription « Vesuvinum » to distinguish it from wines from any other sources.

Scholars of ancient times like Diodorus Siculus, Strabone and Vitruvius were aware of the volcanic nature of Vesuvius. Seneca and Pliny the Elder could have studied it scientifically, but the former died in 65 A.D., and the latter perished in the famous eruption. There were further eruptions in 202, 472, 512, 635, 993, 1036 and 1139, after which the volcano was silent, and the whole surface was covered once again with forests and cultivated areas, until in December, 1631, her re-awakening was so violent that all cultivation and houses were destroyed, and there were thousands of human victims. From that year numerous other eruptions followed, causing damage and alteration to the mountain itself, then after 1906, when the lava flow stopped a few feet short of the Torre Annunziata, the others were of minor proportions until the more alarming one of 1944.

**A VISIT
TO THE EXCAVATION**

**1. - Porta Marina e Antiquarium - Porta Marına and the
    Antiquarium.**

The entrance to the excavations is normally by the Porta
Marina, so called because it faces the sea. There are two
« fornices » (the fornice is the space defined by an arch),
one was meant for pedestrians, as it was less steep, the
other for animals. The niche on the right contained the
statue of Minerva, protective goddess of the gates. A few
steps on, to the right, is the entrance to the Antiquarium,
or Museum, but we suggest that visitors should not linger
here, where we shall return later, but should go on to the
actual entrance hall of the Museum, in order to trace the
historic devolopment during the various phases of its life.
Everything we shall see has been found during excavations.
and exemplifies in the smallest detail the civic and everyday
way of life of the ancient inhabitants.
Since we are at the entrance we are looking straight
over the terrace, which gives a beautiful panoramic view
of the roads and the mountains of Castellamare. Down the
stairs, on the right in a recess between the building and
Porta Marina, the « Lararium of the Pompeians » has
been assembled, and here can be seen busts of the three
famous archeologists who directed all their study and
scientific investigations towards Pompeii: Giuseppe Fiorelli, Michele Ruggiero and the German Augustus Mau. In
recesses on the northern wall various inscriptions record
the history of the principal Pompeian discoveries from
1748 to 1948, and also give the names of those who

directed the excavations. On the far wall, carved on slabs of travertine, is the large topographic map of Pompeii (scale 1 : 400) which is a record of the bicentary commemorated in 1948; and on that same occasion the *Antiquarium*, which had been rebuilt, was opened. Started in 1861, it was destroyed in 1943 by bombing which also struck un-earthed buildings which Professor Maiuri and his skilled workmen were able to restore with rediscovered materials. From the Museum terrace can be seen a stretch of the encircling walls dating from the Samnite period (4th. century B.C.) which can be recognized by the characteristic construction of parallelepipida blocks. On the flat space above and below the walls stood the magnificent « extramural » villa of Porta Marina, but it was destroyed in the earthquake of 62 B.C. Today only a small section of the portico, of the dining and living-rooms can be found. If you have time go down and look at what little remains of its wall decorations, which show the greatness and beauty of this aristocratic dwelling. Now we return to the Museum and begin the visit. It should be mentioned that not everything that has come to light at Pompeii is in the Antiquarium; many works such as murals, mosaics etc. have been preserved on the site of the diggings, while others are kept in the Archeological Museum at Naples. This applies particularly to statues, portraits in bronze, plate, and artistic and historic high-relief, which constitute rare and useful specimens for scholars and those interested in the study of the ancient world of Rome. Because of the brevity of this guide it should be noted that here and elsewehere we will point out only the most important things; so that when the visit is over the tourist can claim to have seen the best of ancient Pompeii.

ENTRANCE: In the centre is a table on « trapezefori » (brackets in sculptured marble, for supporting a horizontal plane). On the walls are decorative sculptures, amongst which should be noted the « Satyr with Club » and « Eros with a Shell ». On the walls there are also mural maps showing the chronological development of the excavations from 1748 to 1948.

FIRST ROOM: Dedicated to the Pompeii of the pre-Samnite epoch, it displays all that has been discovered concerning the primitive period both of the city and the country around the valley of the Sarno. The furniture is displayed

ANTIQUARIUM:
Eros with a shell.

ANTIQUARIUM:
Golden Vénus.

in show-cases placed opposite one another: in cases 1-6, the funeral trappings of the Iron Age, the Etrusco-Campanian « bucari », and bronze ornaments. In cases 2-5 is a lovely series of architectural terracottas which date from the most ancient past of the city; there are fragments of sculpture and painted glass from the facing of the Doric temple of the Tri-angular Forum and the Temple of Apollo, decorative

ANTIQUARIUM: Cast of the dead body of a young woman.

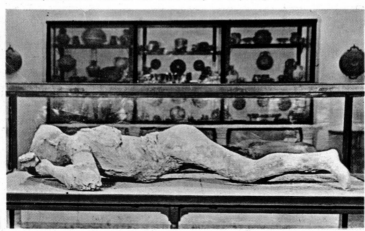

Porta marina. ▶

pediments, friezes, fragments of Greek vases with black and red designs. All these give evidence of the customs, habits and cults, and of the existence of major monuments at that time.

SECOND ROOM: This display illustrates Samnite Pompeii in the phase in which it enjoyed a certain political independence in the first period, while in the second the Greek influence in art, culture and worship can be noticed. On the walls, gracious figured capitals (the capital is the part at the top of the column), and in the space in the passage look at the « Sphinx »by an Italo-Campanian sculptor. On one side is the beautiful capital which has on one part, girded with ivy, the figure of a Maenad (the Maenads were the women who belonged to the retinue of Dionysius) and on the other « Winged Eros ». On the opposite side is another capital with a bust of « Maenad with Timpanum » and « Satyr with Reed-pipe ». On the left-hand wall we can admire the pediment and the altar of the Dionysiac sanctuary, which were found in 1947 near the railway station.

ROOM OF LIVIA: In the centre is the statue of Livia, which used to be an object of worship, and was found in the Villa of the Mysteries. In the corners are portraits of Cor-

HOUSE OF THE VETTII: Boy on a chariot drawn by dolphins.

ANTIQUARIUM: Cast of the dead body of a dog.

nelius Rufus and Vesonius Primus, then the illustrated
« trapezoforum »: « Silenus holding in his arms the Infant
Bacchus ». Opposite, a portrait of Marcellus, nephew of
Augustus.

THIRD ROOM: Dedicated to Roman Pompeii, this room
contains domestic furniture. In the centre are two basins,
the brass one having been found in the House of Menander.
In the corners bronze statuettes of cupids, which came
from the House of the Vettii. In Showcase No. 8, various
types of bronze plate, and a series of bone hair clasps.
Outside this case the very beautiful « situla » (vase for
carrying liquids) with small palms and griffins, which was
found in the House of Menander. In Case No. 9, a series
of ornaments in gold, bone and carved ivory; No. 10;
statuettes of divinities; No. 11, a statue of Pan; and
domestic furniture found in the House of Paquius Proculus
and P. Cornelius Tegete, and in Case No. 12 is an
extremely interesting trousseau in gold and silver. In the
passage are several striking casts of human corpses in
attitudes of self-defence against the terrible death by
asphyxiation. The beautiful body of a young woman, semi-
nude, can be seen, supine, with her head resting on her
arm, and a watch-dog, chained up outside the House of

29

ANTIQUARIUM: Imprint of a mule-driver crouching in a vain attempt to escape.

Vesonius Primus, trying with an extraordinary and dramatic effort to escape from its chain and flee.

FOURTH ROOM: This also is dedicated to Roman Pompeii, but this collection illustrates particular and interesting aspects of the commercial life of the city. Look at Case No. 13. with the work-tools of a bronze and silver-worker; Case No. 14, maritime equipment which was found when the beach of Pompeii was explored; Case No. 15, ingredients of work-shops and shops; Case No. 16, the remains of food, the bread for the oven of Modestus, which is charred, but still enables us to see the shape of the bread, prepared and ready to be cooked; Case No. 17, various mechanical contrivances like locks, hinges, taps, clasps, scales, and a good example of a heating appliance; in Case No. 18, a series of surgical instruments; coins and silverware, found in the big gymnasium, belonging to the people who were fleeing. In the centre a model of a rustic house with the equipment for a wine business.

It is now time for us to return to the entrance of Porta Marina, to the stall where souvenirs of Pompeii are for sale, and where there are more clay models: notice the

View of the Forum.

cupboard, the wheel, the tree, and the mule-driver wrapped in his rough cloak in an effort to save himself from the shower of fire and ashes.

2. - Tempio di Venere - Temple of Venus.

As soon as we come out of the Antiquarium on our way to the « exhumed » city you will note a Pompeian oil-mill for olives on your left, and further on, stop at the first gate on the right, from which you can see the area where stood the temple dedicated to Venus, protectress of the city. Ruined by the earthquake, it had not yet been restored at the time of the famous eruption; and little remains of the primitive temple.

3. - Il Foro - The Forum.

This was the heart of the political, religious and social life of Pompeii, around which were constructed the various public buildings which we are going to see. The large rectangular piazza (square), is 38 metres wide and 142 metres long; and at the time of its destruction it must have been surrounded on three sides by a big arcade, on top of which was an open gallery, supported by smaller columns, and on the fourth side was the Temple of Jupiter. To the south can be seen a section of « trabeation » (this is the part overhanging the columns and consists of architrave,

Street in the Forum.

frieze and cornice) from the Samnite era, while the columns and trabeations of the eastern and western sides date from the Roman period. On the southern side of the arcade are several pedestals on which at one time were collected the statues of worthy citizens; on the western side there was a much larger pedestal which was the tribune of the orators. It takes little to imagine how magnificent this square must have been, with the great arcade covered with precious marbles, with the solemn statues, and the whole area paved in travertine, and surrounded by splendid public buildings. Above all we think of it as the lively centre of public life - a meeting-place for citizens of every class, and for farm-labourers from the hinterland controlled by Pompeian administration.

4. - Tempio di Apollo - Temple of Apollo.

On the western side of the Forum is the *Temple of Apollo*, but before entering we shall walk further along the arcade itself, where almost at the end of the aforementioned temple, in a niche in the outside wall, we can find the « mensa ponderaria », the office which used to standardise the measures of capacity with those of the Roman system. A little further on, a row of pillars in brick mark the building which could very easily have served as a storehouse for cereals; and at the end in the corner to the left, a large latrine, and, shortly afterwardes, two underground rooms which, it seems, were used for the municipal treasury. Turning back, we now enter the Temple of Apollo, which already existed in the Samnite epoch, but was later dedicated to that divinity (6th. century). In the Roman period substantial modifications were made according to the architectural and decorative concepts of that time. As we can see, it had a portico of 48 columns, and in front of the stairs is the *ara*, the altar (which in Greek and Roman temples was always in an open space in front of the temple); to the left of the stairs, on top of an Ionic column is a sun-dial constructed at the expense of the « duumviri » L. Sepunius and M. Erennius. At the top of the stairs there is a Corinthian colonnade of six columns along the front, and the entrance to the « cella », which constitutes the innermost part of the temple where the images of the divinity were kept. As we turn back, before descending the stairs, notice the arcade in front, and the bronze statue of Apollo to the left, and that of Diana to the right. These

Temple of Apollo.

Basilica

are copies, the originals of which can be found in the Archeological Museum at Naples.

5. - Basilica.

The most important public building in Pompeii, this served for the administration of justice, and for the meetings of business-men who gathered here to discuss their affairs. The building is rectangular, measuring 24 metres wide by 55 metres long, divided into three aisles by great brick columns, with at the back two rows of columns, which betray the influence of Greece. It has been extremely difficult for historians to establish the date of the foundation of this building, but the recovery of various tiles bearing the Iscan seal, and tests made in the foundations have led to the conclusion that it was perhaps constructed about the year 120 B.C., that is in the pre-Roman period.

6. - Uffici municipali - Municipal Offices.

Beside the Basilica are the three rooms where the *Municipal Offices* were situated, and where the « duumviri », the aediles and the Municipal Council were based. The central room must have served as the public archives, and in the larger room the council meetings were held. All these areas must originally have been covered with marble slabs.

Eumachia Building.

7. - Comizio - Comitium.

On the Corner of Via dell'Abbondanza is the *Comitium*, where the elections for public offices were held. Proceeding on, turning right into the Vico dei Dodici Dei. we find the *Casa del Cinghiale - House of the Wild Boar*, so called because on the floor is depicted in mosaic a wild boar being attacked by two dogs. The whole house is interesting for its decorations in marble and mosaic, beautiful examples of which are in the hall, and the busts on medallions in the tablinum. Behind is a large portico with a garden, on the southern side of which is a spacious exedra for meetings and for conversation.

8. - Edificio di Eumachia - Building of Eumachia.

On returning to the Comitium we find the Building of Eumachia, which takes its name from the inscription over the door facing Via dell'Abbondanza, and on the porch facing the Forum, which says that the cost of construction of the building was borne by the priestess Eumachia. It was to be the seat of the Corporation of the « Fullones », which consisted of cloth-makers, launderers and dyers. Eumachia dedicated the place to Concordia Augusta and to « Pietà » (both personifications of Livia, wife of Augustus). The Corporation of Fullones, important for the number

37

FORUM: Detail of the Portico.

porch stretches the « cryptoporticus », a closed arcade which was used as a promenade, and to connect with other buildings. Here was found the beautiful statue of Eumachia which the Fullones had made as an acknowledgement. The statue is now in the Archeological Museum at Naples.

Portico of the « Macellum ».

of its associates, had a significant influence on the commercial and political activities of the city. We enter on the Forum side: the facade has a double row of columns, and a very beautiful rectangular doorway of marble, decorated with spirals of acanthus leaves. Through this entrance is a spacious courtyard, with three apses on the far side, the middle contaming the statue of the Empress. Behind the

9. - Tempio di Vespasiano - Temple of Vespasian.

This was dedicated to the worship of the imperial cult. Note the beautiful « ara » in marble, with a relief representing a scene of sacrifice. One can see the sacrificing priest, the « victimarius » (who leads the victim to the altar), the lictors, a flute-player, and young ceremonial ministers. In a shrine at the back is a statue dedicated to the cult.

10. - Santuario dei Lari - Sanctuary of the Lares.

After the famous earthquake of 62 B. C. this sanctuary was built in atonement and dedicated to the protective gods of the city.

11. - Macellum.

This was a covered market used for the sale of foodstuffs, especially meat and fish, and its construction dates back to the imperial era. In front, looking out onto the Forum, is an elegant porch of marble columns, and it was here that the money-changers did their business. Inside is another porch which collapsed during the earthquake of 62, and in the centre a circular construction with a water-basin, while beyond there were places dedicated to imperial worship. On the right is the place that was reserved for the sale of fish. Also the Macellum had been decorated with mosaics of mythological designs, and perhaps around all the walls was a frieze portraying various kinds of foods.

12. - Tempio di Giove - Temple of Jupiter.

Dedicated to three divinities, Jupiter, Juno and Minerva, this temple derives from the 2nd. century B.C., and constituted the Capitol of Pompeii. It must have been a beautiful and imposing structure, fronted by a double flight of steps and with a « pronaos » (atrium surrounded by columns) crowned by Corinthian columns. Inside was a large « cella » in which was found an enormous marble head of Jupiter, which is now in the Archeological Museum in Naples. Half destroyed by the earthquake, it was in the midst of being restored at the time of the catastrophic Vesuvian eruption. At the side are two honorary arches dedicated to the imperial family, perhaps to Tiberius and Germanicus.

View of the Forum from the Arch of Germanicus.

BATHS OF THE FORUM: Room of the « Tepidarium ».

13. - Terme del Foro - Forum Thermal Baths.

Passing through the arch to the right of Jupiter's Temple, we find the Refreshment-room for those wishing food and drink. Opposite are the Offices directing excavations, to which those studying the subject may refer for incidental information. Straight after this, to the left, at No. 12 Via delle Terme, is the entrance to the Forum Thermal Baths. They are not on a large scale, but can give us an example of how an important public service was organized, specially since they have remained for us in an excellent state of preservation. The baths are divided into two sections: one for men and one for women. A small corridor leads into the men's changing-rooms; note the niches for clothes and the seats where the men could await their turn in the bath. From here they entered the « frigidarium » (where they had cold baths in a tub) which is decorated in stucco-work. Returning to the changing-room, on the left is the entrance to the « tepidarium » (the room between the hot and cold baths) with the barrel vault decorated in stucco, and niches in the walls adorned with « telamones » (human figures which are used in architecture to support trabea-tions and cornices) in terracotta. Note the brazier used to heat this area, which was constructed at the expense of Marcus Nigidius Vaccula. From the « tepidarium » they would enter the « calidarium » (bath-room for hot baths or « Turkish » baths), with a double wall for the passage of hot air, and a large bath-tub, on the side of which are inscribed in letters of bronze the names of the donors, who had it placed there in the years 3 - 4 O. D.: « Cnaeus Melissaeus Aper and M. Staius Rufus ». The bath cost 5240 sestertii (Roman coins of silver, but which were of bronze during the imperial period, and weighed one ounce). Also one should not overlook the stuccoes on the ceiling. These baths, which also boasted a gymnasium, were constructed in the initial period of Roman colonization, in 80 B.C.

BATHS OF THE FORUM: Room of the « Calidarium ».

Temple of the Dea Fortuna Augusta.

HOUSE OF THE FAUN: Atrium and Tablinium. ▶

14. - Tempio della Dea Fortuna Augusta - Temple of the Goddess Fortuna Augusta.

It was dedicated to the imperial cult, and was constructed in the year 3 B.C. by Marcus Tullius, an important personage in Pompeii, a military tribune elected on numerous occasions to public office. One reaches the temple by a staircase with an « ara », coming to the pronaos decorated with six Corinthian columns, and in the small inner area, at the back, there is the « cella » which contains the shrine with the inscription of the donor. On the side walls are niches for statues.

15. - Casa del Fauno. - House of the Faun.

Turning right out of the Temple of the Goddess Fortuna, into the street of the same ,name. we shall find at Nos. 2 - 5 the *House of the Faun*. In the impluvium was found

a beautiful small bronze representing a dancing faun (the Latin pastoral god): hence the name of the house. The bronze we can now see is a copy, and the original is in the Archeological Museum at Naples. We find ourselves in front of one of the largest and most sumptuous dwellings of the Samnite era (2nd. century B.C.), but every one of the architectural elements betrays Greek and Italian influences. Precious mosaics have been removed from this house, and are now housed in the aforementioned Naples Museum, and amongst the most famous of these is the « Battle of Alexander ». As you enter, the greeting *Have* (Hail) welcomes you. In the hall the floor is coloured marble, and on the walls a « polychromy » (number of colours) is painted to represent a marble facing, and high up are two Lararia executed in stucco. Next is the grandiose atrium with valuable decorations on the walls, and off this open the alae, paved with mosaic; beside the tablinum are the dining-rooms, then the small tetrastyle atrium, then the first peristyle composed of twenty-eight Ionic columns, and a big basin with a fountain. At the back is the exedra, on the floor of which was the famous « Battle of Alexander ». From here and from beyond the exedra are other triclinia, to the right of the peristyle the domestic quarters (kitchen, bath and a stable) and along a corridor is another very large peristyle with a garden.

Leaving the House of the Faun, on Via della Fortuna, we find at No. 59 the *Casa della Parete Nera - House of the Black Wall*, the name of which comes from a spacious room behind the peristyle which contains very pretty panels of Cupids inserted in a wall on a black back-ground. At No. 57 is the *Casa dei Capitelli Figurati - House of the Figured Capitals*, a beautiful house of the Samnite period, with pillars at the entrance with finely worked capitals with Bacchic figures, and beyond, in the garden, there is a sun-dial and the sacellum of the Lararium. At No. 48 is the *Casa della Caccia - House of the Hunt*, an interesting dwelling of the pre-Roman period, but which has just inside the entrance reconstructions in the fourth style. In the atrium are representations of the seasons « Winter » and « Autumn », beautiful paintings on mythological subjects in the cubiculum and the right wing, while on the walls at the bottom, of the garden is the large fresco which gave its name to the house: a beautiful countryside with scenes of hunting wild beasts.

16. - Casa del Poeta Tragico - House of the Tragic Poet.

If you have time, before visiting the House of the Tragic Poet, go under the *Arco di Caligola* in Via del Mercurio, along which you go only a short way to find, on the right at No 7, the *Casa dell'Ancora - House of the Anchor*, so called because of the mosaic at the entrance which represents an anchor. Above all you should see the lovely garden, in

HOUSE OF THE TRAGIC POET: The Portico.

HOUSE OF THE TRAGIC POET: « Beware of the dog ».

the lower part of which are apsed niches, while the upper part in enclosed by a rather graceful colonnade. At No. 1 is the *Caupone* or *Osteria - Tavern*, with a typical example of a Pompeian shop counter, with a « repositorium » for the kitchenware and the cooking. while further inside is the meeting-place for clients, decorated with paintings in the

HOUSE OF THE FAUN: Faun dancing.

HOUSE OF THE GREAT FOUNTAIN: Nymphaeum and mosaic.

popular style, portraying various aspects of tavern life - note the « Four Drinkers sitting at the Dinner Table ». Across the street, at No. 23 is the *Casa della Fontana Piccola - House of the Little Fountain*, and at No. 22 the *Casa della Fontana Grande - House of the Great Fountin..* In the first is a fountain with a niche in mosaic made of a glass paste, and a statuette of a young boy with a goose (a copy, the original of which is in the Archeological Museum); also a graceful « nymphaeum » (temple of nymphs, and in this case a fountain consecrated to nymphs). Notice on the walls the valuable landscape composition in mosaic, with a

Arch. of Caligula.

beautiful polychromatic effect. In the second house is another graceful fountain decorated with mosaics and bronze statuettes, the originals of which are in the Archeological Museum. At Nos. 20 - 21 a spacious « Fullonica », or place for washing and dyeing clothes, with suitable accommodation.

Going back under the Arco di Caligula. we find to the right the *House of the Tragic Poet*. In the tablinum was found a mosaic representing a theatrical producer, for lyric or tragic theatre, and this gave the house its name. But the house is more famous for the various frescoes of heroic an mythological topics (amongst which the Sacrifice of Iphigenia), which were found on the walls of the atrium and peristyle, and have been placed in the Naples Museum. It is familiar to the general public because the writer Bulwer Lytton describes it as Glaucus' house in « The Last Days of Pompeii ». The house belonged to a citizen of the middle classes who became wealthy through his activities as a merchant, which can be seen by the two shops beside the entrance. Notice here the mosaic depicting a watch dog with the inscription « cave canem » (beware of the dog), and in the atrium the marble basin of the impluvium; around it are the various cubiculae and the staircases which go up to the first floor rooms. Beyond the tablinum is a small porch with a garden, at the bottom of which is the Lararium. To the right of the porch, after the kitchen, is the dining room of the triclinium, the walls of which are painted with the following mythological subjects: « Venus contemplating a nest of Cupids » above « Mars and Olympus », « Theseus abandoning Ariadne » and « Dido and Aeneas »; and on the side panels representations of the « Seasons ».

17. - Casa di Pansa - House of Pansa.

Grandiose house of the Samnite period, belonging to Cnaei Allaei Mai, but converted by the last owner, who divided it into apartments for hire, and on the Vicoli della Fullo-

HOUSE OF PANSA: The Peristyle.

HOUSE OF THE SMALL FOUNTAIN: Fountain and Mosaic.

Bakery and grindstones in the « Crooked Lane ».

nica and di Modesto there are numerous shops and places for hire. Nothing has remained of the primitive decoration. Through the entrance is the atrium and the usual impluvium, the tablinum and the peristyle with a large pool in the middle, and further on a spacious living room. Beyond is the orchard, today used for a plant nursery.

18. - Casa di Sallusto - House of Sallust.

From the House of Pansa take the Via Consolare, where at No. 3 is the house of the baker, with his equipment for making bread. At No. 4, the House of Sallust from the Samnite period, which belonged to A. Cossii Libani. Here too there are shops bordering the entrance, while inside is a large atrium in the Tuscan style with an impluvium on the same scale; in the tablinum and in one cubiculum are still preserved examples of wall-painting of the first stile. Very different is the decoration of the small peristyle with hexagonal columns on the southern side in post-Augustan style. In the « gineceo », the place reserved for women, on one wall was painted the myth of « Actaeon surprising Ariadne at her bath », but this work was destroyed by bombing in the second World War.

The Herculaneum Gate and Burial Way.

19. - Casa del Chirurgo - House of the Surgeon.

Further along on Via Consolare at No. 13 is a building called « Statio Saliensium », where it is presumed there was a salt warehouse, and the Guild of those attached to the salt-works found along the coast. At No. 10 is the solid facade of the *House of the Surgeon*, so called because here were found surgical instruments, of inestimable value for the study of ancient surgical equipment. The collection is in the Archeological Museum. Furthermore, the house is an excellent example of the limestone period dating back to the 4th. and 3rd. centuries B.C. Shortly after is the *Casa delle Vestali - House of the Vestals*, which is interesting for its elegant entrance-hall; then we come to the Porta Ercolano, beyond which starts the Via dei Sepolcri, which we shall see when describing the suburban Villas. The Porta Ercolano, which was first called « Porta Saliniensis » consists of three arches, the middle one for carriages and the two side ones for pedestrians. It was certainly constructed in the times of the Roman colony, on top of one from a previous era.

20. - Casa di Meleagro - House of Meleager.

From Porta Ercolano follow the inside of the solid city wall, and take the fourth street which is the Via del Mercurio. At No. 24 we find the *Casa di Apollo - House of Apollo*, the facade of which is true to the Italic type, but inside has decorations from a later Pompeian period. Behind the tablinum notice the lovely fountain, and in the garden a cubiculum with on its walls a mosaic of « Recognition of Achilles at Scyros », which is a landscape. Inside are paintings of the fourth style, with scenes showing the « Music Contest between Apollo and Mars ». Opposite, at No. 2, the *House of Meleager*, a beautiful aristocratic dwelling of the Samnite period, but which contains inside decoration typical of the fourth style. Above all one should admire in this house the beautiful architecture of the peristyle, in the centre of which is a large garden pool with statuettes. To the right of the peristyle there are three large rooms; the central one has an arcade in Greek style, and must have been a luxurious reception-room. Beyond this is the imposing triclinium with very rich decorations, but this has unfortunately very much deteriorated. Next door, at Nos. 3-5 the *Casa del Centauro - House of the Centaur*, an area composed of three buildings; the cubicula to the right

is interesting, as it has on its walls decorations in the first style. Opposite, at No. 18, the *Casa di Adone - House of Adonis*, which is worth visiting for the beautiful painting on the garden wall depicting « Venus with the wounded Adonis », while in a room on the southern side a decoration of the third and fourth styles consists of paintings where the « Toilet of Hermaphrodite » is depicted.

Going along Via del Mercurio to Nos. 6-7, we enter the *Casa di Castore e Polluce - House of Castor and Pollux*. Here note the magnificent atrium with twelve Corinthian columns, and beyond the tablinum the porch with a shrine. To the right of the tablinum a room is decorated with paintings representing « Birth of Adonis », « Scilla and Minos »; to the left are « Apollo and Daphne », and « Silenus with nymph and the Infant Bacchus ». On the right side of the atrium is a peristyle with a basin in the middle, and on the walls pictorial decorations of the fourth style. A short way along Via del Mercurio turn right into Vicolo di Mercurio, where at No. 10 is the *Casa del Labirinto - House of the Labyrinth*, a noble house from Samnite times. The name derives from a design in the pavement of one room, which opens onto the large peristyle. A mosaic depicts the « Myth of Theseus and the Minotaurs in the Labyrinth ». The house has two halls, the principal in tetrastyle, the other in Tuscan style. Beyond the large peristle are the reception rooms, the middle ones with a Corinthian colonnade, beside the room containing the mosaic with the myth of Theseus. The western side had been converted for commercial use, as we can see from the equipment for an oven and a mill, while beyond is a private bath.

21. - Casa dei Vettii - House of the Vettii.

To visit this luxurious abode follow the numbers on the plan we have included on page 13. This gives an illustration of the aristocratic Pompeian home. The one we are going to visit now used to belong to two merchants, probably brothers, whose business was very prosperous: Aulus Vettius Restitutus and Aulus Vettius Conviva. In the construction of this splendid house, however, they did everthing they could to deny their origin as merchants; they felt they were gentlemen and wished to be considered as such.This house can provide for the visitor a truly complete image of the Pompeian Roman house of the

HOUSE OF THE VETTII:
Dedalus and Pasifaë.
(North-East Oecus).

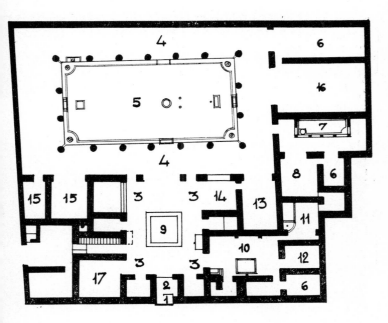

HOUSE OF THE VETTII.

1. - Vestibulum
2. - Fauces
3. - Atrium
4. - Peristyle
5. - Garden
6. - Cubicula
7. - Peristyle
8. - Triclinium
9. - Impluvium
10. - Hall with a Lararium
11. 12. - Kitchen
13. - Triclinium
14. - Alae
15. - Oecus
16. 17. - Triclinium

HOUSE OF THE VETTII: The Garden.

HOUSE OF THE VETTII: The Triclinium.

HOUSE OF THE VETTII: The Peristyle.

wealthy classes, especially when we consider it was built almost entirely after the disastrous earhquake of 62 A.D. Besides the arrangement of the rooms, the House of the Vettii enjoys world-wide fame for the copious wall decorations in the fourth style. Intelligent excavation has permitted the reconstruction of the whole building, in its entirety, by means of restoration and re-touching, so that there is a genuine atmosphere of a home which should impress the visitor.

We enter the hall (1), where there is (covered) an obscene painting of Priapus, god of fertility. The superstitious

HOUSE OF THE VETTII: Cupid on a crab.

HOUSE OF THE VETTII: Wall frescoes.

Vettii had had it painted so that it would protect them from the evil-eye of those envious of their prosperity. (The picture can be seen on request by adults only.) Then through the fauces (2) we enter the hall (3) with the impluvium (9) in the centre to collect the water which falls from the roof; on the sides are two strongboxes where money and silverware were kept, and on the pillars and the plinths beautiful figures of cupids and maidens. In the small room to the left of the entrance (2) a frieze of fish in a pond can be found, with underneath two small paintings « Ariadne deserted » and « Hero and Leander ». In the room next door (17) there are some others, much larger: « Mourning Ciparissus » « Pan and Love fighting » above « Jupiter enthroned » and « Leda and Danae ». Also in the atrium are the two wings; the one on the left has panels with « Cockfighting », while the right-hand one (14) shows medals, small yet expressive, with the heads of « Medusa » and « Silenus ». To the right of the atrium (10) is a small hall with a Lararium like a temple, decorated in stucco, and there is a painting of the « Genius », head of the family, between two Lares, and underneath a serpent in an attitude of acceptance of the funeral offerings. No. 12 is the room for cooking, and at No. 11, in a small courtyard, is the kitchen, whose hearth contains a trivet and a cauldron in bronze. Opposite the kitchen is another

HOUSE OF THE VETTII:
Dedalus and Pasiphaë.

HOUSE OF THE VETTII:
Hercules a boy.

small room with obscene pictures shown only to adults. From here we move to the women's quarters (8) with a triclinium and an elegant little portico (7). Now we come outside into the large peristyle (4) which encloses a beautiful garden with flower-beds, statuettes in bronze and

HOUSE OF THE VETTII: Cupids.

HOUSE OF THE VETTII: The sacrifice of Iphigenia. ▶

HOUSE OF THE VETTII: Cupids.

HOUSE OF THE VETTII: Cupids.

marble, with basins brimming with water. The interesting thing to notice in this garden is that it was not designed deliberately, but during excavations it was found that ancient water conduits underneath faithfully followed the lay-out of the garden, as it had been laid out by the Vettii, who were able to see the peristyle and the garden in all its colourful beauty from the large triclinium (16) where lighthearted symposia used to be held. On entering this room we must admire the wall decoration, which is on a red base, divided up by pilasters with black bands. Each square must have had in the centre a painting on the theme of dining, but nothing has remained of this decoration, while on the lower part, on a cornice above the plinth, a delightful series of Cupids can be seen, executing various tasks. From right to left: Cupids aiming stones at a target, some intertwining and buying flowers; some absorbed in preparing and selling perfumed oils; the chariot race; Cupid metal-workers and goldsmiths; some following the trade of fullers, some celebrating the Vestalia; some gathering grapes; the triumph of Bacchus, and Cupids selling wine.

Under the frieze of Cupids, between the pilasters, are panels with « Psyches ». In the central squares of the long walls are panels with mythological subjects: on the right-hand wall « Agamemnon about to kill the Sacred Hind » and « Apollo slaying the Python », while on the left are « Orestes and Pylades before Thoas and Iphigenia ». On the side walls mythological romantic couples: « Perseus and Andromeda », « Dionysius and Ariadne », « Apollo and Daphne », « Poseidon and Amymone ». Leaving the large triclinium we go into the smaller one (13) with lovely wall paintings: on the left « Dedalus showing Parsiphae the Wooden Cow », opposite « Issione tied by Vulcan onto the Wheel, in the presence of Juno », to the right « Epiphany of Dionysius and Ariadne ». On the other side of the atrium, in the largest room, numbered No. 15, on the left is « The Infant Hercules strangling the Serpents » and opposite « Pentheus being torn to pieces by the Bacchantes » and on the right « The Torture of Dirce ».

HOUSE OF THE GOLDEN CUPIDS: The Garden.

22. - Casa degli Amorini Dorati - House of the Golden Cupids.

This was the aristocratic dwelling of Cnaeus Poppeus Abitas, and its name derives from the decoration in the cubicula, the walls of which depict Cupids engraved on gold foil. Here we find ourselves in a house which is an example of the house of a noble family of the Neronian period. Through the entrance, paved with the mosaic « Leda with the swan and Narcissus at the Fountain » is a cubiculum to the right, while to the left is « Mercury in Fligth ». On the back wall of the tablinum is a representation of « Paris and Helen at Sparta ». From the hall we pass into the elegant peristyle, the western side of which is raised, owing to the unevenness of the terrain, and this results in a beautiful scenographic effect. Between the columns hang the so-called « oscilla », or marble discs with various designs; on the southern wing can be seen a delicately finished fragment of marble with « Silenus » and other fragments. Between the atrium and the peristyle is the triclinium, the walls of which display pictures of the third style: to the left « Thesis in Vulcan's Workshop », on the back wall « Jason, wearing only one Sandal, before Pelias », to the right « Achilles and Briseis and Patroclus in the Tent ». In the centre of the western porch is a large

HOUSE OF THE GOLDEN CUPIDS: The Peristyle.

HOUSE OF THE GOLDEN CUPIDS: Venus fishing. ▶

triclinium, with a small room on either side — in the right-hand one are mural paintings « Diana and Actaeon, Leda, Venus Fishing ». In the northern porch, near a big room decorated in black is the cubiculum with the Cupids. The House of the Cupids faces onto Via di Stabia, whose paving-stones are deeply scored by the continuous passing of carriages. At the end, on the left, is Porta Vesuviana; one of the most important in the city; which was damaged in the earthquake, and at the time of the great eruption was in the middle of being restored. Next to it is the distributor of dater supplied from a branch of the aqueduct from Serino.

23. - Casa di Orfeo - House of Orpheus.

Returning from the Porta Vesuviana along Via di Stabia, after the House of the Cupids, at No. 28 is the *Bisca*: *Gambling-House*, with an emblem of a vase on the facade, between two obscene pictures. This was where the dice-players and the young of both sexes gathered, and the proprietor must have been able to make a large profit from their loans. At No. 21 is the Fullonica, a laundry and dyers which has been converted into an aristocratic home. At No. 20 the *House of Orpheus*, which used to belong to Vesonius Primus, and was built in the Samnite period, but was almost entirely rebuilt in the imperial era. The name comes from the large mural on the back wall of the peristyle which shows « Orpheus amongst the Wild Beasts ». From here was taken the plaster cast of the chained dog which we saw in the Antiquarium.

24. - Casa di Lucio Cecilio Giocondo - House of Lucius Caecilius Jucundus.

Opposite the House of Orpheus, at No. 26, is the *House of Lucius Caecilius Jucundus*, well known by scholars not only for its beauty but for the important material that was found which provided information about bank book-keeping. In fact during excavations a box was unearthed in which were perfectly preserved some wax tablets (on which the Romans used to write with a stylus) which were receipts, and also a beautiful and life-like portrait in bronze of the owner of the house, who was an experienced and well-known banker. The portrait on display is a copy - the original is in the Archeological Museum. A wise administrator, Caecilius Secundus wanted a beautiful home. Note that the marble reliefs of the Chapel of the Lares, in the hall on the left, have a votive character: one represents the « Temple of Jupiter and the Triumphal Arch » of the Forum, the other « Porta Vesuviana with "tripartitore" of water collapsing after the earthquake ». The « erma » (pillar bearing the head of a man; the name erma derives from the fact that the god Hermes was originally represented thus) next to the tablinum was erected by a loyal freedman (a freed slave) whose portrait is on top, and in the tablinum one of the most beautiful decorations in the third style can be detected, although it is in bad condition.

Leaving the house of the bankers, we come to the Quadrivio di Orfeo - Cross-roads of Orpheus, then on the left, at No. 21, the *Casa del Torello - House of the Young Bull.* The beautiful facade dates back to the Samnite period, and in the entrance you can see the ingenious method adopted to disappoint the glances of prying passers-by: the double door in which a smaller door gave access to the house. On the wall at the back of the peristyle are what remains of a nymph, in three niches, between pilasters faced with mosaic, from whence water used to spring, to be collected in the basin below.

25. - Casa delle Nozze d'Argento - House of the Silver Wedding.

Proceeding along Via di Nola we ocme to No. 1: the *Casa della Regina Margherita - House of Queen Margaret,* with beautiful pictures in the rooms along the sides of the tablinum. To the left are « Leda and the Swan », « Poseidon and Amymone », « Jupiter and Danae », « Meleager and Atalanta »; to the right « Narcissus », « Ariadne Deserted » and « The Madness of Lycurgus ». Taking the small lane to the right, next to this house, we come to the *House of the Silver Wedding,* whose name derives from the fact that it was excavated in 1893, the year during which the sovereigns of Italy celebrated their Silver Wedding. This beautiful patrician house dates back to the Samnite epoch, but both the structure and the decorations were modified in the imperial age. One's initial impression; on entering, is of a dignified grandeur; there is an imposing tetrastyle entrance hall with enormous Corinthian columns, and it is decorated in the second style. Through the atrium

Street of the Augustali.

is the peristyle, the most luxurious part of which is towards the south: there are four columns supporting the ceiling of the impressive rom, whose walls are painted with architecture of the second style. In the ambulatory there are cubicula decorated in the same style, and one room with black walls, and there is a private bath, with a calidarium and a tepidarium; and in the garden a tub for cold baths.

26. - Casa di Marco Lucrezio Frontone - House of Marcus Lucretius Fronto.

In this small house of the imperial era we can enjoy the pictorial decoration, which has been delicately and expertly carried out in the third style. In the tablinum, besides the panels on rural themes, there are two small paintings: « The Wedding of Venus and Mars » and « The Triumphal Pomp of Bacchus ». In the large triclinium is « Neoptolemus killed by Orestes at Delphi » and in a room to the right of the tablinum « Narcissus at the Fountain » and « Perõ feeding her old father Micone ». To the right of the atrium « Theseus and Ariadne » and « The Toilet of Venus », and on the wall at the bottom of the garden is a lovely representation of scenes of the hunt.

27. - Casa dei gladiatori - House of the Gladiators.

With the construction of the Amphitheatre the Pompeians became excessively fanatical about gladiatorial games; and it was for this reason that this house was converted for the gladiators' use. The peristyle is decorated with hunting scenes and mythological designs, and on the colums can be seen the scratched inscriptions which every gladiator used to love making, to boast of his exploits in the ring and also with women. As we go out, to the left we see Porta di Nola in the distance, with its single arch, from the Samnite era. At the top of the arch is a head of Minerva.

28. - Casa di Obellio Firmo - House of Obelli Firmi.

A lovely house from the Samnite period, with a double hall and a double entrance. The larger atrium is tetrastyle, and in the impluvium is a charming statue of a Satyr (a cast, the original being in the Archeological Museum) and to the right the Lararium and a strongbox. Behind the peristyle is a large room and a cubiculum, decorated with paintings of the second style.

Love Punished. (Naples, National Museum).

29. - Casa del Centenario - House of the Centenary.

So called because it was discovered in 1879, the eighteenth centenary of the famous eruption. The building consists of three dwellings, and underwent various transformations in the imperial period, before and after the earthquake of 62. Worthy of note are the spacious Tuscan entrance hall, its mosaic floor, and the impluvium. The walls are decorated with pictures of the fourth style on theatrical subjects.

A fine view of the Forum.

On either side of the tablinum are two rooms with graceful decorative themes, and from there is the entrance to the peristyle, on the walls of which are yellow panels bearing the emblems of Juno, Apollo and Minerva. In the garden there is a pool, in which was found a very graceful little bronze of a « Satyr with Wineskin » (now in the Archeological Museum) and « Bacchus at the Foot of a Mountain Covered with Forests and Vines ». In this Vesuvius has been recognised, as it was before the eruption. There is also a bath; and several rooms, in one of which there are three small paintings, on a black ground: « Theseus and the Minotaur », « Hermaphroditus and Silenus » and « Orestes, Pylades and Iphigenia », and there is also a room with erotic drawings which is closed to the public.

30. - Terme Centrali - Central Baths.

We have already seen the lay-out of the Forum Baths, but those we are about to enter constitute the most modern version of the Roman thermal bath, since they were constructed after 62 A.D., in accordance with the dictates of the most exacting taste of those times. Unfortunately they were never completed. These baths covered a whole « insula », that is, one of the blocks into which the urban area was divided, and to the north and east there are numerous shops. The main entrance is from Via Stabiana, and opens immediately into a large palestra, and on the far side can be seen the « natatio », the swimming pool, and to the south the latrine and changing - rooms. On the eastern side is another large dressing-room; the tepidarium and the laconicum, the place for « Turkish » Baths, is circular, with a cupola, then the calidarium, with apsed and rectangular niches, and in the walls windows have been hollowed out, to provide light. This is a new feature, and together with the laconicum shows us the difference in construction and lay-out from the previous baths.

31. - Casa di Marco Lucrezio - House of Marcus Lucretius.

On Via di Stabia at No. 5 is the House of Marcus Lucretius, a Pompeian citizen of some note, who was in fact a « decurione » (in charge of a decuria in the Roman cavalry) and a priest of Mars. His house was consistent with his dignity of office: in the atrium, on the right is the Lararium, opposite a large tablinum; and behind, the garden rises upward, where you can admire the beautiful fountain, as well as niches and lawns in which are collected hermae in marble and some attractive statues representing « Silenus with a Wineskin », « Satyrs », « Pan », « Cupid riding a Dolphin », and figures of animals. The house used to contain beautiful paintings of the fourth style, most of

HOUSE OF MARCUS LUCRETIUS: The Garden.

which have been removed and placed in the Archeological Museum, but the paintings on the tablinum remain: « Triumph of Bacchus followed by a Satyr and Carriage ».

32. - 33. - 34. - Casa di Gavio Rufo, Forno di Modesto e Casa dell'Orso - House of Gavius Rufus, the Bakehouse of Modestus, and the House of the Bear.

The *House of Gavius Rufus* deserves a fleeting glance, although it differs from the others only to a slight degree, but most interesting is the bake-house of the baker Modestus, with its millstones made from two pieces of volcanic lava, the lower one in the form of a full cone, the upper one like a hollow double cone. On the top was the rotation

81

Portico of the « Macellum ».

axis which by means of a frame-work of boards and two projecting shafts, used to grind the wheat. The machine was worked by slaves or by donkeys. The *House of the Bear* has in the entrance a beautiful figured mosaic, and a graceful fountain, also decorated in mosaic, at the end of the peristyle.

35. - Albergo di Sittium - The Lodging-House of Sittius.

This modest lodging-house belonged to a certain Sittius. There were two entrances and displayed outside was a « For Rent » notice for a triclinium with three beds, in relative comfort. Opposite this house is the Lupanare, the house of prostitution, of two floors, with small rooms decorated with designs and obscene sketches. At No. 47 in Vicolo del Lupanare is the *Casa di Sirico - House of Siricus*, consting of two communicating apartments with another entrance in Via de Stabia. These must have belc.iged to two rich merchants, Siricus and Nummianus, perhaps brothers or associates in the same business. The house on Via del Lupanare must have been intended for commercial dealings, for on the floor of the entrance is written « salve lucru(m) ». In the triclinium there are paintings on the wall portraying « Neptune and Apollo », « Hercules Inebriated »

Stabian Baths.

and « Thetis with Vulcan ». In the section facing the Via di Stabia the following are of interest: the Tuscan atrium; the marble impluvium; the fountain and the table, which is supported by two « trapezofori », and at the back of the portico the triclinium is decorated with scenes of Cupids; and the paintings represent « Orestes and Pylades », « Mars and Venus », and « Diana and Endymion ».

36. - Terme Stabiane - Stabian Baths.

The entrance is in Via dell'Abbondanza. These baths date back to the times of the Roman colony, and have undergone numerous alterations in the course of time, especially in the decoration which belongs to the imperial period. After the 62 earthquake restoration was begun, but was not completed because of the eruption. We enter a large palestra or gymnasium, with columns in plaster on three sides; immediately to our left is the men's section of the vestibulum, which is decorated with stucco illustrations, and next is the changing-room with a *lacunari* vault (ceiling in the form of squares or losenges) of stucco with war trophies and other designs. Through here went those desiring the frigidarium, reaching it by returning to the vestibule. It is circular, with a cupola roof, and decorations on the walls portraying sea fauna and shells. Returning to the changing-room, in the far left-hand corner of the room is the entrance to the tepidarium, which was heated with hot air coming from a space under the floor. From here we enter the beautiful apsed room with a bath-tub for ablutions, hot or cold: the calidarium. Note the lovely stucco frieze which encircles the walls. To see the women's section we must return to the palestra and go back through the area we have already visited. Straight outside the vestibule turn right, where almost at the end of the colonnade a passage leads to the dressing-room; the tepidarium and the calidarium.

On the north side of the palestra is the oldest section, which, consisted of various small rooms with entrances in the Vicolo del Lupanare. The western side is from the last period — notice the open-air swimming-pool with along the sides rooms for changing, and for oiling, with oil and sand; all these facilities were available to those participating in various sports: wrestling, boxing and gymnastic exercises.

37. - Casa di Cornelio Rufo - House of Cornelius Rufus.

Opposite the Stabian Baths is the *House of Cornelius Rufus*, which contains two beautiful « trapezofori » and an impluvium worthy of note. Next turn into Via de Stabia, and at the corner turn right into Via del Tempio di Iside, and opposite is the *Tempio di Giove Melichios - Temple of Jupiter Meilichius*, where homage was paid to Zeus Meilichius, whose Greek pre-Roman cult was very probably imported from Sicily. Note the beautiful altar in tufo. Nearby is the *Tempio d'Iside - Temple of Isis*, from pre-Roman times but reconstructed at the expense of Popidius Celsinus after the earthquake of 62. It is surrounded by high walls, and its original structure is preserved. Beside the staircase is a great altar, and the tabernacle has a high podium with a pronaos and a small rectangular cella. In the corner of the peristyle to the southeast a small temple containing stucco decorations given access to a tiny underground cavern in which was kept water from the Nile. Behind the temple is a large hall, meeting-place for the followers of Isis, and a short distance away the houses where the priests lived. After the Temple of Isis, continuing along the street, of the same name, we come to the *Palestra Sannitica - Samnite Gymnasium*, which is a small rectangular space defined on three sides by a colonnade of the Doric order. It was constructed in the Samnite era by the quaestor Vibius Vinicius, and was used for sporting competitions by the young Pompeians from the patrician and wealthy classes.

38. - Foro Triangolare - Triangular Forum.

The name comes from its geometrical shape, and here the Greek influence is more marked than anywhere else. One enters the Triangular Forum through the extremely beautiful « propylaeum » (monumental vestibule with columns) which consists of six Ionic colomns (only four are visible, with a public fountain in front). The extensive square has, on three sides, a portico composed of 95 Ionic columns, and in front of the entrance is the pedestal where once stood the statue of Augustus' nephew, Claudius Marcellus. Almost in the centre are the the remains of a Doric temple which was dedicated to the cult of Hercules and Minerva. This temple is what remains from the period in which Pompeii was under the hegemony of the Cuman State.

Triangular Forum.

39. - Caserma dei Gladiatori - Gladiators' Barracks.

This grandiose quadruple portico was not originally for gladiators, but was a meeting-place for the numerous spectators who crowded into the Great Theatre, which we will see shortly. During pauses in the performances they used to stroll here, discussing what they had seen. In Nero's time it was converted into quarters for the gladiators taking part in the displays, and they used to live here with their families and practise for the gladiatorial contests. The living-area for the families was spread over two floors at the edges of the four porticoes, and it was here that were found the fascinating and beautiful weapons which are now on display in the Archeological Museum.

40. - Teatro Grande - Great Theatre.

This very beautiful theatre was constructed in accordance with Greek tecniques of architecture in the period between 200 - 150 B.C., and enlarged by the architect M. Artorius in the time of Augustus on purely Roman lines. The architect knew how to profit from the natural space offered by the hill, and he constructed there the « cavea massima », the flight of steps reserved for the spectators (of which a few of the lower steps can be seen) and which he managed to make large enough to accommodate five thousand people.

Gladiators' Barracks.

41. - Teatro Piccolo - Little Theatre.

This was a covered theatre particularly devoted to musical and prose performances, and its capacity would not have been more than a thousand. It was built between 80 and 75 B.C. by the magistrates G. Quintus Valgus and Marcus Porcius. Well-preserved in the « cavea massima », it gives us one of the most beautiful examples of ancient theatrical architecture. Going out into the Via di Stabia we can see at the end the *Porta di Stabia*, one of the most ancient in the city, which is made rather picturesque by luxurious vegetation, and beyond the gate are a number of tombs.

42. - Casa di Menandro - House of Menander.

This is one of the loveliest and most interesting houses in Pompeii, and it owes its name to a portrait there of the Greek poet Menander. The house used to belong to a patrician family, and the owner was Quintus Poppeus. Here in 1930 was found a real treasure of silverware, consisting of 115 pieces, which are now in the Archeological Museum. In the atrium can be seen pictorial decorations of the fourth style, the Lararium in the form of a small temple, and an exedra to the left has paintings of mythical subjects: « The Horse of Troy », « The Death of Laocoon », « The Meeting in Priam's Palace of Menalaus and Helen ». Then after the tablinum comes the grandiose peristyle with columns

The covered Theatre.

in red and black; to the north is the triclinium with two oeci: in the right-hand one is the frieze painted with « Centaurs and Leucippids ». On the southern side is a series of apsed and rectangular exedrae, with portraits of poets and hunting-scenes, and on the western side is a

HOUSE OF THE EPHEBE: Statue of the Ephebe.

beautiful bath-room with a calidarium decorated with mosaics and pictures. From the bath-room a corridor leads to the kitchen and cellars, and in one of these was found the set of silverware which had been placed here because the house was being restored. In the same block the *Casa degli Amanti - House of the Lovers* is worthy of note: it has a delicately decorated atrium, a peristyle with two rows of columns, with a garden, and in the vicinity of the luxuriously decorated portico is a small painting where a hexameter in Latin reads as follows; « Lovers, like bees, suck sweet life like honey ». In all probability the house was lived in by those in comfortable circumstances and by young newlyweds.

43. - Casa del Citarista - House of the Citharist.

At No. 5, Via di Stabia, is the spacious *House of the Citharist*, so called because a bronze statue (now in the Archeological Museum) of « Apollo the Citharist » was found here. An aristocratic dwelling which dates back to the Roman period, it must have been made up of the joining of two houses, because there is a double atrium. and three peristyles. The pictorial decoration has beer. removed and placed in the Archeological Museum.

HOUSE OF MENANDER: Atrium of the tourist quarter.

44. - Casa del Criptoportico - House of the Crypto-porticus.

The interest here lies in the « cryptoporticus » which can be reached by descending a small flight of stairs, and traces of decoration in the second style can be seen. The barrel vault is faced with stucco and decorated with floral motifs, and all round there is a large frieze with « Scenes from Various Episodes of the Iliad ». Here in special show-cases are plaster casts of those who took refuge in the crypto-porticus from the eruption, but who died from asphyxia-tion. In the triclinium are decorations in the second style, with cariatids, small pictures and still life. In the same block the *Casa di Lucio Ceio Secondo - House of Lucius Ceius Secundus*, with a beautiful facade covered in stucco, and through the vestibule the copies of two doors and the re-stored painted ceiling. From the tetrastyle atrium a small staircase leads up to the second floor, where there is another model of a cupboard. In the garden a single composition showing Egyptian influence hase been painted on three walls. Straight after this the *Fullonica of Stefanus*, a house converted into a laundry, with all its equipment. To the right of the atrium is the Lararium, decorated with fine

HOUSE OF THE CRYPTOPORTICO: Casts of two dead bodies.

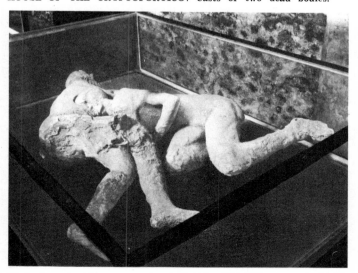

work, and on its roof a frieze on a blue ground which reproduces episodes referring to the last canto of the Iliad.

45. - Casa di Paqui Proculo - House of Paquius Proculus.

The owner was an influential personage, in fact his name recurs in various electoral programmes. In the vestibule is the image of a dog chained up; the tablinum and triclinium are decorated with beautiful mosaics. In an exedra on the north side of the peristyle were the skeletons of seven infants who had hidden there from the eruption. Next door to this house is the *Casa dell'Efebo - House of the Ephebe*, so called because a statue in bronze of an Ephebe was found here, but moved to the Archeological Museum. The large area is made up of three apartments joined together, and particularly worthy of note is the triclinium with the couches and the marble inlay in the floor, and in the garden the Lararium and a painting of « Mars and Venus ». Now glance briefly into the *Casa del Sacerdote Amandus - House of the Priest Amandus*, which is at No. 7 in Via dell'Abbondanza. There is an interesting triclinium with paintings of the third style showing « Polyphemus and Galatea », « Perseus and Andromeda », « Hercules in the Garden of the Hesperides », and « Dedalus and Icarus ».

Goblet with parrots and a dove. (Naples, National Museum).

Paquius Proculus and his wife. (Naples, National Museum).

Hercules and Telephus. (Naples, National Museum)

Shop sign of M. Vaecilius Verecundus in the Street of Abundance.

46. - Officina Verecundus - The Verecundus Workshop.

This is one of the most typical of the Pompeii workshops, where dress-materials and felt objects were manufactured, and clothes were made. Above the interesting facade is the roof, and beside the entrance are four paintings: two are dedicated to the divinities protectors of workshops; there are « Mercury and Venus of Pompeii in a quadriga drawn by four elephants », then the scene of « Boiling done by Textile-workers and Felt-workers », then another two scenes of « Selling at the counter ».

47. - Cenacoli e Termopolio di Asellina - Refectories and Thermopolium of Asellina.

Two long open galleries formed by columns and pillars constituted the refectories which originally were to contain textile workshops and their proprietors' dwellings. Next door is the *Thermopolium of Asellina* which is a direct ancestor of the modern bar, where hot and cold drinks were sold. Exacavations have unearthed it for us in its entirety, complete with crockery in terracotta and in bronze. Notice the oil-lamp hanging from the ceiling, the urn for the drinks and the small board with round notches in varying sizes, used to keep the money received from clients. Beyond, on the outer face of the thermopolium we see written women's names: Asellina, Aegle, Maria and Smyrna, names which imply a lot; we can assume that the clients were not insensible to the charms of these young

STREET OF ABUNDANCE: **Thermopolium of Asellina.**

girls attached to the shop and the tavern on the second floor. Leaving the Thermopolium of Asellina, after a block we come to the *Casa di Caio Giulio Polibio - House of Caius Julius Polibius*. Originally from the Samnite period, it has undergone various alterations for commercial reasons, however it is interesting to read on the side wall a poem scratched in Latin by a melancholy poet. Translated it reads thus: « Nothing in the world can endure in perpetuity. Now the Sun shines clearly, now it sinks into the ocean. The moon is half-gone, which shortly before appeared full..., Thus every feather obeys the wind, the most cruel denial of love ».

Opposite the House of Polibius, on the Via dell'Abbondanza, are the latest excavations. At No. 1 is the aristocratic *Casa del bell'impluvio - House of the Beautiful Impluvium*, the entrance to which is through a shop. After the earthquake it was in the midst of being restored. Particularly admirable are the atrium and the tablinum; in the former the impluvium is decorated in mosaic in polychromatic marble, and in the latter are wall decorations of the third style, on a blue ground. At No. 3 is the *Casa di Successus - House of Successus*, where in a cubiculum to the left of the atrium is a mural representing a « Frightened putto attacked by a duck ». On the painting is inscribed « Successus »; from whence came the name of the house. Under the small portico in the garden is a statuette of a naked boy with a pigeon, serving as a « trapezoforum ». At No. 5 the *Casa del Frutteto - House of the Orchard* which one enters

HOUSE OF LOREIUS TIBURTINUS: Garden.

through a shop which must have belonged to a fruit-grower, since in the various cubicula of his house can be found painted, in the third style, a lovely series of fruit trees which the owner used to cultivate in his orchard.

48. - Casa di Trebio Valente - House of Trebius Valente.

Before the Second World War this house was famous because the facade was completely covered with large mural inscriptions, referring to elections, performances at the Amphitheatre, announcing the names of the entrepreneurs of the various champions of the gladiatorial games, eulogies on the champions themselves, and various notices. Today nothing remains of these inscriptions, which were destroyed during military operations. The interior of the house is interesting, with a most effective chess-board design in the peristyle, an out-door triclinium under an arbour with water playing, and a beautiful cubicula with paintings of the second style.

49. - Schola Armaturum.

This large area was the base of a large military organization, and this fact dictated the style of decoration. On the outside pilasters are trophies of war, and on those inside is the recurrent motif of stylised candelabras surmounted by military emblems. From impressions on the wall it can easily be seen that there was between the pillars a series of partitions where were kept weapons for display and for training. At the end of the neighbouring lane is the *Casa di Pinario Ceriale - House of Pinarius Ceriale* where an artist of note must definitely have lived who was an expert in the art of engraving and carving precious stones, ivory and cameos, for in his house were found 114 stones, cut and uncut. The two-floored house has in the garden portico a theatrical scene from the tragedy « Iphigenia in Tauride ». Returning to the Via dell'Abbondanza, next to a tavern at Nos. 2 - 3 are two communicating houses which belonged to T. Arrius Polites and M. Epidus Hymenaeus, who must have been related. The house of the latter has been known as the *Casa del Moralista - House of the Moralist* because of three great paintings in the triclinium, which is situated under an open gallery of the floor above. The walls show, painted in white on a black ground, precepts which the owner of the house wished to be observed:

Flora gathering flowers. (Naples, National Museum).

1) « The servant shall wash and dry the feet of the host; a napkin must protect the cushions (of the bed) and our linen must be well cared for. 2) Abandon lascivious looks, and do not cast sweet glances at the women of others, be chaste in speech. 3) Abstain from anger and contumely if you can, if not return to your home ».

50. - Casa di Loreius Tiburtinus - House of Loreius Tiburtinus.

A patrician home, this house has a large doorway with brass studs, through which we enter the rectangular atrium elaborately decorated on a ground of red, white and

HOUSE OF LOREIUS TIBURTINUS: **Biclinium.**

102

yellow. Beyond the atrium and the peristyle there is a loggia or long open gallery, and a portico with a pergola, and in the centre a small tetrastyle temple. Then there is a canal bordered by marble statues with designs of animals and Muses, and at the end the triclinium with two signed paintings (Lucius pinxit) representing « Narcissus » and « Pyramus and Thisbe ». On another side of the loggia is another triclinium, decorated with a frieze of « Scenes from the Iliad » and « Episodes from the Legend of Hercules ». On the western side is a cubicula which gives us one of the most perfect examples of the fourth style, on a white background: amongst the various figures and medallions note the figure of a priest of Isis with an inscription (amplus alumnus Tiburs) which may be recognized as a portrait of one of the members of the patrician family.

51. - Casa di Venere - House of Venus.

The name derives from a monumental mural painting executed on the wall at the bottom of the garden, which was found in 1952. In it is portrayed « Venus of the Sea escorted by Cupids », which cannot be described as a masterpiece, but the artist has managed to obtain a naturalistic and colourful effect of some worth. On the left is an image of Mars, and in a cubiculum on the right side of the atrium there is a medallion with « Young Citharist » and a « Still Life ».

52. - Casa di Giulia Felice - House of Giulia Felice.

This covers the area of a whole block and was completely uncovered in 1952-53, although it was first excavated in 1755-57. The name of the proprietress was easily discovered because on one of the entrance doors was a « For Rent » notice which mentioned her name. It is now in the Archeological Museum. This very large place is made up of three parts: the house of the owner, on Via dell'Abbondanza, and on the same road a public bath, a tavern and area for rental. In the eighteenth century the building underwent some pillage, for example from one room in the north-east corner were taken nine figures of Apollo and the Muses, which are now in the Louvre in Paris. It must have been a beautiful garden with the

HOUSE OF VENUS: Fresco with birds. ▶

Armodius and Aristogitones.
(Naples, National Museum).

The Amphitheatre.

colonnade and fish-pond decorated with sculptures in marble and terracotta; amongst the latter is a terracotta representing the Greek tyrant Pittacos. Under the western portico is the triclinium, which was decorated with a valuable frieze of « Still Life » now in the Archeological Museum. The bath-room has more or less the same features as those we have already seen, with a dressing-room, rectangular frigidarium, tepidarium and Laconicum with a cupola, here used only for « Turkish » baths. At the end of this street is the *Porta di Sarno*.

53. - Anfiteatro - Aphitheatre.

This was constructed in 80 B.C. by the same builders who made the Little Theatre, and it can be considered as the oldest amphitheatre which has come down to us. The impressive elliptical shape, with its giant flight of stairs, could hold 12.000 spectators, and it is 135 metres long and 104 metres wide. At the top of the steps can be seen great rings of stone, which were used to support the framework of the « velarium », a type of awning which was spread out over the spectators to protect them from the sun or the rain, and also for acoustic reasons. There are no underground rooms.

Mercury resting.

(Naples, National Museum).

Satyr sleeping.

(Naples, National Museum).

54. - La Grande Palestra - The Great Palestra.

Opposite the Amphitheatre is the large Palestra (gymnasium) which was excavated berween 1936 and 1951. It presents a quadrilateral space girt on three sides by porticoes, with a large swimming pool in the centre. Here the young Pompeians used to come and train for athletic games and their chosen sports. The area is 130 by 140 metres, and the pool was surrounded by two rows of large plane-trees, to provide relief from the heat and the sun and traces of the roots of these trees can be seen.

55. - L'orto dei Fuggiaschi e Porta di Nocera - The Orchard of the Fugitives and the Porta di Nocera.

If you have time, go from the northern part of the Palestra, and after a block you will come to Via di Porta di Nocera where it intersects the Via dell'Abbondanza. Here new excavations have brought to light shops and houses designed for commercial business: amongst the most

Water -jar (hydria) with Apollo and Marsias.
(Naples, National Museum).

The great Palaestra.

important are the *Termopolio della Fenice - Thermopolium of the Phoenix* with an orchard and a pergola with vines, the *Officina del Garum - Workshop of the Garum*, where they prepared a famous sauce of this name, made from sea-water and the entrails of certain types of fish. Turning back into the right-hand block on the corner of Via Nocera is the *Casa del Larario di Sarno - House of the Sarnus Lararium*, a modest house which, however, has told us something of how maritime business was conducted in Pompeii. In the courtyard the Lararium is in the form of a small temple, with a painting in popular style showing the loading of farm products onto a small boat. Going down Via Nocera, a lane to the right leads to the *Casa degli Archi - House of the Arches*, a lovely house where for the first time can be seen in the garden portico the architectural motif of an arch built on columns. Further along Via Nocera are the fortifying walls; turn right here, and in the second block will be found the *Orchards of the Fugitives,* discovered in 1961 behind the portico of a rustic house with an orchard. Here, in the layer of ashes, were found the remains of thirteen victims of the eruption: adults, children and babies. When you turn round you will see the Porta di Nocera, built before Roman times, but later restored by them. Outside the gate, along the fortifying wall have been collected the casts of the victims found in the neighbourhood, and beyond, the Necropolis, excavated a short time ago, where there is an interesting collection of commemorative monuments, among them that of Eumachia, who had constructed in the Forum the building for the Corporation of the Fullones, and also those of numerous other magistrates and military tribunes.

NEW POMPEII

Leaving the excavations by the Amphitheatre entrance, on the left is the beginning of the built-up area of new Pompeii; a small town which occupies an area which was inhabited even after the famous eruption of 79 A.D.; called Campo Pompeiano, it has undergone many vicissitudes during the past centuries. A church dedicated to the Saviour was built there, and a castle which belonged to Caracciolo. The whole area was feudal territory which was passed from hand to hand, changing with the political situation of the Kingdom of Naples. In 1873 the lawyer Bartolo Longo) 1841-1926), a religious and charitable man, became the prime mover among the people devoted to the Most Holy Rosary, and founded the Sanctuary of the « Madonna of the Rosary », around which he built, with the help of the faithful, charitable institutions and orphanages. The Sanctuary soon became a centre of fervent worship, famous for its worship of the Virgin. Many pilgrims from all over Italy convene here, usually in the summer and autumn.

In the main square is the imposing Sanctuary, by the architect Antonio Cua, which was begun on May 8, 1876 and consecrated on May 7, 1891. It was enlarged in a second period between 1933-39, the project of the engineer Spirito Chiappetta, and the facade was designed by Giovanni Rispoli, who conceived it as two architectural orders: the lower, Ionic, and the upper Corinthian. Above the middle of the papal loggia (the Sanctuary bears the title of a Basilica, and the Rector Archbishop is appointed by the Pope) is the marble statue of the Madonna of the Rosary by the sculptor Gaetano Chiaramonte. To the left of the facade is the large bell-tower, constructed between 1912 and 1925 by the architect Aristide Lenori. It is 80 metres high, consisting of five floors, which are reached through the lovely bronze door. At the four corners of the third floor there are four angels in bronze, and the belfry with eleven bells. In a niche on the fourth floor is a gigantic statue of the Sacred Heart of Jesus, and at the top is a terrace surmounted by a large cross. From the terrace (which can be reached by a lift) there is a superb view - one can see old and new Pompeii, Vesuvius, the sea, the valley of the Sarno and various mountains.

The interior of the Sanctuary is very rich. It is on the plan of a Latin cross with three aisles, and everywhere there is a great quantity of precious marbles which create a luminous polychromatic effect, and in the cupola there are frescoes, and on the walls mosaics. In the middle is the main altar with the venerated image of the Virgin of the Rosary, surrounded by myriads of precious stones. It

is interesting to visit the Treasury, which is entered from the left-hand aisle, and consists of precious religious furnishings. There is a table, a « Saint Paul » attributed to Fra Bartolomeo, a candelabra by Vincenzo Ierace for the Easter candles, portraits of Popes, benefactors and founders.

The square communicates with the square of the Municipio, where to the left is the Via Sacra. Here are the « Terme Forte Salutare »: Fountain of health-giving springs, from which comes a spring composed of cold alkaline bicarbonate which, with mud-baths, is most effective against rheumatism, asthenia, exhaustion and metabolic disturbances.

The fine façade of the famous Sanctuary.

115

THE SUBURBAN VILLAS

56. - Villa di Diomede - Villa of Diomed.

A visit to the excavations at Pompeii would not be complete without seeing the *Villa of Diomed* and the very famous Villa dei Misteri. They can be reached by car or cab, or on foot it is just under a kilometre from Porta Ercolano. Outside this gate starts the Via dei Sepolcri, which was unearthed between 1763 and 1938. It is a road about half a kilometre long, with along its sides beautiful sepulchres ·from Greek and Roman times, but which every now and then leave spaces for the porches of taverns and villas. The general effect along the whole distance is singular; the variety of architectural forms of the patrician homes, of the more or less wealthy classes, of porticoes and villas make a deep and memorable impression.

The brevity of this guide precludes our stopping to admire, as we ought, the various burial-grounds, so we shall pass through them quickly to the Villa of Diomed. This majestic suburban dwelling came to light in 1771-74, when it evoked considerable interest because of the discovery in an underground portico of eighteen victims of the eruption. Hardly anything remains of the sumptous decorations, but several of the paintings can be found in the Archeological Museum. However it is very interesting to explore the sections of which it is composed, as they give us an idea of the lay-out of an aristocratic villa built outside the city. From the entrance one can see the large peristyle, to the left, divided into five areas, the bath with portico and the swimming-pool. Then on the southern side of the peristyle we enter a room which leads into another

116

VILLA OF THE MYSTERIES

in the shape of an apse, with three windows. This alcove was perhaps a place of sojourn, where the sun and light could be enjoyed in the morning of the afternoon. Going from the alcove towards the tablinum, we enter from here a loggia with an open terrace where the inhabitants used to stroll and take the sun. This terrace is situated above the portico, from which we can descend by a staircase and a ramp to the largest garden in Pompeii, which used to be enclosed by four porticoes, in the corners of which stood small towers which commanded a beautiful view of the sea. In the centre of the garden is a large swimming-pool and a summer triclinium, with a fountain. After leaving the villa it is a short distance to the wall enclosing the excavations, and immediately past the door-keeper's house in the Viale della Villa dei Misteri.

57. - Villa dei Misteri - Villa of the Mysteries.

We find ourselves before a massive square building, which in all consists of some sixty rooms. The grandiose Villa of the Mysteries is so called because in one of the rooms was found a pictorial masterpiece which portrays, it is thought, the initiation of brides to the Dionysiac mysteries. The villa was discovered in 1902, excavated between 1909-10, and almost entirely restored between 1929 and 1930. Here we find collected together from different sources, in foundation all the functional, architectural and decorative elements of Pompeian life. We are indebted to the famous Professor of Archeology Amedeo Maiuri for the most detailed knowledge of this extraordinary and monumental building, especially in the field of painting, of which he made a profound critical study, which has become an indispensable reference book for scholars. A complete description of the Villa would take many pages, so we shall limit ourselves just to a visit to the famous hall of paintings.

From a large semi-circular exedra with windows flanked by roof-gardens, we go straight into the original tablinum, which was converted into an ordinary room. Here note the beautiful miniature wall decorations on a black background in the Egyptian style. From the tablinum one enters a cubicula containing paintings of the second style, amongst which should be noted the malicious figure of the « Dancing Satyr », thence through a small door into the

VILLA OF THE MYSTERIES: **The Catechesis** (detail).

VILLA OF THE MYSTERIES: The reading of the Ritual.

VILLA OF THE MYSTERIES: Bacchante kneeling, winged demon, the woman scourged, and nude bacchante.

VILLA OF THE MYSTERIES: **The Sacrifice and Silenus playing**
the lyre.

VILLA OF THE MYSTERIES: **Terrified woman and Silenus with satyrs.**

room with the famous painting. If it is your first visit you will be overwhelmed by the magnificent scene on the wall, and will be captivated by the peculiar mystical atmosphere, by a sense of mysterious meditation, notwithstanding the fact that the subject depicted is unrelated to associations of a religious order as we know them today. There is a lively controversy as to the meaning of the whole composition, and scholars are unable to give us a

VILLA OF THE MYSTERIES: The Sacrifice and Silenus playing the lyre. (detail).

definite explanation; however the prevalent current opinion is that it portrays « The Initiation of Brides to the Dionysiac Mysteries ». This cult of Dionysius was widely spread throughout Campania and Etruria, and even reached Rome, but its definitely orgiastic and obscene character provoked severe sanctions by the Senate against its followers. For that reason the cult was practised in private by only a few initiates. At the Villa of the Mysteries the

« domina », or lady of the house, was an initiate or priestess of the Dionysiac rites, which she celebrated in the utmost secrecy in this triclinium. She commissioned a Campanian artist who lived in about the middle of the first century B.C. to paint this remarkable composition, in the second style, which unfolds along the walls enlivened by 29 figures of a natural grandeur, divided into groups, each of which is participating in one of the sacred or profane moments of the Dionysiac rite.

The picture should be viewed from left to right: 1) Initiation with the reading of the ritual by a young boy; 2) The sacred agape, with a young girl holding a dish with offerings; 3) Silenus playing his lyre, and a pastoral scene; 4) Terrified woman fleeing from the sight of a winged demon which is lashing her companion; 5) Silenus with Satyrs; 6) The Marriage of Dionysius and Ariadne; 7) Bacchante kneeling in the act of lifting a drape which covers the symbol of peace and fecundity; 8) Woman scourged, and nearby a nude female Bacchante dancing, as a prey to the mystic exaltation; 9) Toilet of a bride preparing herself for initiation to the Mysteries; 10) Woman sitting covered in a mantle - this is very probably a portrait of the lady of the house, the priestess of Dionysius.

The great frieze, designed so as to unfold along a single plane, betrays the hand of a great artist who knew how to create a monumental effect in the whole of his composition, which is carried out on an even background of a dark red colour, by means of a small variety of colours, amongst which the predominant colours are yellows, greens and violets The various groups are articulated in a rhythmical treatment worthy of a great painter of the classic era, so much so that it is probable that this artist must somehow have been influenced by that period. His pictorial language is rich, his plastico-linear solutions are such that this work must be considered one of the greatest masterpieces of the ancient world.

Finito di stampare nel marzo 1973